Circle Time Songs

by Ellyn Marciano

To my loving and supportive family,
I thank you dearly for your thoughtful contributions,
perspectives and insights!

Circle Time Songs

ISBN: 9789659322305

This book belongs to

____

Circle, Circle

Shake, Shake, Stop

Three Little Apples

Two Elevators

I Like My House

Circle Circle

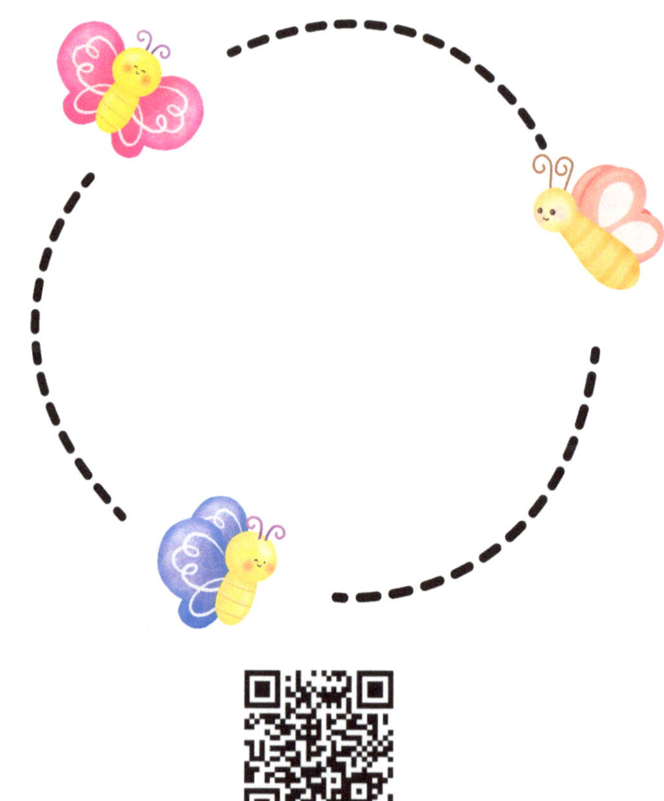

Circle, circle ‘round the sun,

shining down on everyone.

Circle ring and circle ball.

Circle raindrops
where they fall.

Circle moon and circle dime.

Sitting down for circle time.

Circle, circle ‘round the sun,
shining down on everyone.

Shake, Shake, Stop

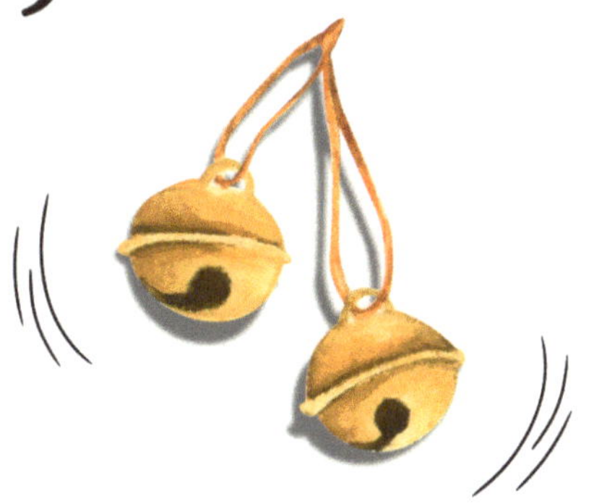

Shake, shake, STOP.

Shake, shake, STOP.

Shake on the bottom

Shake on the top.

Shake, shake, STOP.

Shake, shake, STOP.

Shake your little bells with me.

Three Little Apples

Three little apples

Sweet, golden apples
just for me.

One after breakfast,

one after tea.

One little apple on my tree.

Three little birds came,

Sweet, golden birds
upon my tree.

One sang a song

and one flew free.

One ate the apple
from my tree.

Two Elevators

Two elevators

in the middle of town.

One going
UP
and
one going
DOWN.

and STOP!

5
4
3
2
1
and STOP!

Two little trains on the railroad track.

One going forward,

One going back.

1 2 3 4 5
and STOP!

5 4 3 2 1
and...

STOP!

I Like My House

I like my house.
My house is wide.

Wide is my house
from side to side..

I like my kitchen.

My kitchen is bright.

Bright is my kitchen.
Warm and bright.

When I take a bath
I'm in my tub.

That's where I like to
play and scrub!

I like my room
and my big bed

That's where I lay
my sleepy head.

Other books by Ellyn Marciano

Parker Pelican

If I Were...

Uh-Oh: A Silly Rhyming Song

About the author 

Ellyn Marciano began writing poetry and making up songs from the age of 6. Her favorite themes were "make-believe" and the everyday life of the young child. As an adult, Ellyn continued to write and perform songs for young children. Now, as a retired teacher, Ellyn has put her creative efforts into producing fun, imaginative books for children that acknowledge the special connection young children have with their inner circle of family and friends. Each thoughtfully crafted story-song book appeals to every child's imagination, sense of adventure, and love of music, rhyme and silliness! The books are also meant for adults, who can enjoy reliving this magical time as they read the stories and sing along with their children and grandchildren!

About the illustrations

All of the illustrations for Ellyn's books were created by Ellyn Marciano using the digital CanvaPro® design platform. Each picture is made up of multiple layers of elements from the CanvaPro® gallery which are then extensively edited with effects, and other editing tools. The result is a unique set of whimsical and colorful characters, backgrounds, and scenery with a "hand-painted" feel and which express the writer's artistic vision for each song "story".

About the music 

This series of books is based on the album "Ellyn's Songs", written, and recorded by Ellyn Marciano and produced by Ellyn and Dawn Fintor in 1988. The songs were written by Ellyn and inspired by her life with her own young children and the pre-schoolers she interacted with during her years as a music specialist for young children.

To Parents, Pre-School Teachers, "Mommy/Daddy-and Me" Group Facilitators, English Teachers and Tutors...

Each "song" in this book has a scannable **QR code** on its title page. When scanned with a 'smart' device, it is possible to hear each song in its entirety on your device. There is **no charge** for this feature! The audio tracks on the 'Ellyn's Songs' album are available for free and can be accessed immediately and as often as you like.

Hearing the music along with the book adds another dimension of enjoyment for young children. Repetition and integration of music and movement with language is known to facilitate first and second language learning in young children.

During the years that I was working with, entertaining, and raising my own very young children, I was inspired to write most of the songs on the "Ellyn's Songs" album. I encourage those who work and play with young children to share the songs and pictures during story time and in activity "circle" times, while integrating movement and finger play as suggested by the lyrics. Children will enjoy singing along with the catchy, happy tunes - and so will you!

www.ingramcontent.com/pod-product-compliance
Lightning Source LLC
Chambersburg PA
CBHW042048110726
48006CB00002B/329

* 9 7 8 9 6 5 9 3 2 2 3 0 5 *